EARLY BARDIC

LITERATURE

OF IRELAND.

By Standish O'Grady

BYRNE, A BLIND IRISH HARPER.

Scattered over the surface of every country in Europe may be found sepulchral monuments, the remains of pre-historic times and nations, and of a phase of life will civilisation which has long since passed away. No country in Europe is without its cromlechs and dolmens, huge earthen tumuli, great flagged sepulchres, and enclosures of tall pillar-stones. The men by whom these works were made, so interesting in themselves, and so different from anything of the kind erected since, were not strangers and aliens, but our own ancestors, and out of their rude civilisation our own has slowly grown. Of that elder phase of European civilisation no record or tradition has been anywhere bequeathed to us. Of its nature, and the ideas and sentiments whereby it was sustained, nought may now be learned save by an examination of those tombs themselves, and of the dumb remnants, from time to time exhumed out of their soil—rude instruments of clay, flint, brass, and gold, and by speculations and reasonings founded upon these archaeological gleanings, meagre and sapless.

For after the explorer has broken up, certainly desecrated, and perhaps destroyed, those noble sepulchral raths; after he has disinterred the bones laid there once by pious hands, and the urn with its unrecognisable ashes of king or warrior, and by the industrious labour of years hoarded his fruitless treasure of stone celt and arrow-head, of brazen sword and gold fibula and torque; and after the savant has rammed many skulls with sawdust, measuring their capacity, and has adorned them with some obscure label, and has tabulated and arranged the implements and decorations of flint and metal in the glazed cases of the cold gaunt museum, the imagination, unsatisfied and revolted, shrinks back from all that he has done. Still we continue to inquire, receiving from him no adequate response, Who were those ancient chieftains and warriors for whom an affectionate people raised those strange tombs? What life did they lead? What deeds perform? How did their personality affect the minds of their people and posterity? How did our ancestors look upon those great tombs, certainly not reared to be forgotten, and how did they—those huge monumental pebbles and swelling raths—enter into and affect the civilisation or religion of the times?

We see the cromlech with its massive slab and immense supporting pillars, but we vainly endeavour to imagine for whom it was first erected, and how that greater than cyclopean house affected the minds of those who made it, or those who were reared in its neighbourhood or within reach of its influence. We see the stone cist with its great smooth flags, the rocky cairn, and huge barrow and massive walled cathair, but the interest which they invariably excite is only aroused to subside again unsatisfied. From this department of European antiquities the historian retires baffled, and the dry savant is alone master of the field, but a field which, as cultivated by him alone, remains barren or fertile only in things the reverse of exhilarating. An antiquarian museum is more melancholy than a tomb.

But there is one country in Europe in which, by virtue of a marvellous strength and tenacity of the historical intellect, and of filial devotedness to the memory of their ancestors, there have been preserved down into the early phases of mediaeval civilisation, and then committed to the sure guardianship of manuscript, the hymns, ballads, stories, and chronicles, the names, pedigrees, achievements, and even characters, of those ancient kings and warriors over whom those massive cromlechs were erected and great cairns piled. There is not a conspicuous sepulchral monument in Ireland, the traditional history of which is not recorded in our ancient literature, and of the heroes in whose honour they were raised. In the rest of Europe there is not a single barrow, dolmen, or cist of which the ancient traditional history is recorded; in Ireland there is hardly one of which it is not. And these histories are in many cases as rich and circumstantial as that of men of the greatest eminence who have lived in modern times. Granted that the imagination which for centuries followed with eager interest the lives of these heroes, beheld as gigantic what was not so, as romantic and heroic what

6

was neither one nor the other, still the great fact remains, that it was beside and in connection with the mounds and cairns that this history was elaborated, and elaborated concerning them and concerning the heroes to whom they were sacred.

On the plain of Tara, beside the little stream Nemanna, itself famous as that which first turned a mill-wheel in Ireland, there lies a barrow, not itself very conspicuous in the midst of others, all named and illustrious in the ancient literature of the country. The ancient hero there interred is to the student of the Irish bardic literature a figure as familiar and clearly seen as any personage in the Biographia Britannica. We know the name he bore as a boy and the name he bore as a man. We know the names of his father and his grandfather, and of the father of his grandfather, of his mother, and the father and mother of his mother, and the pedigrees and histories of each of these. We know the name of his nurse, and of his children, and of his wife, and the character of his wife, and of the father and mother of his wife, and where they lived and were buried. We know all the striking events of his boyhood and manhood, the names of his horses and his weapons, his own character and his friends, male and female. We know his battles, and the names of those whom he slew in battle, and how he was himself slain, and by whose hands. We know his physical and spiritual characteristics, the device upon his shield, and how that was originated, carved, and painted, by whom. We know the colour of his hair, the date of his birth and of his death, and his relations, in time and otherwise, with the remainder of the princes and warriors with whom, in that mound-raising period of our history, he was connected, in hostility or friendship; and all this enshrined in ancient song, the transmitted traditions of the people who raised that barrow, and who laid within it sorrowing their brave ruler and, defender. That mound is the tomb of Cuculain, once king of the district in which Dundalk stands to-day, and the ruins of whose earthen fortification may still be seen two miles from that town.

7

This is a single instance, and used merely as an example, but one out of a multitude almost as striking. There is not a king of Ireland, described as such in the ancient annals, whose barrow is not mentioned in these or other compositions, and every one of which may at the present day be identified where the ignorant plebeian or the ignorant patrician has not destroyed them. The early History of Ireland clings around and grows out of the Irish barrows until, with almost the universality of that primeval forest from which Ireland took one of its ancient names, the whole isle and all within it was clothed with a nobler raiment, invisible, but not the less real, of a full and luxuriant history, from whose presence, all-embracing, no part was free. Of the many poetical and rhetorical titles lavished upon this country, none is truer than that which calls her the Isle of Song. Her ancient history passed unceasingly into the realm of artistic representation; the history of one generation became the poetry of the next, until the whole island was illuminated and coloured by the poetry of the bards. Productions of mere fancy and imagination these songs are not, though fancy and imagination may have coloured and shaped all their subject-matter, but the names are names of men and women who once lived and died in Ireland, and over whom their people raised the swelling rath and reared the rocky cromlech. In the sepulchral monuments their names were preserved, and in the performance of sacred rites, and the holding of games, fairs, and assemblies in their honour, the memory of their achievements kept fresh, till the traditions that clung around these places were inshrined in tales which were finally incorporated in the Leabhar na Huidhré and the Book of Leinster.

Pre-historic narrative is of two kinds—in one the imagination is at work consciously, in the other unconsciously. Legends of the former class are the product of a lettered and learned age. The story floats loosely in a world of imagination. The other sort of pre-historic narrative clings close to the soil, and to visible and tangible objects. It may be legend, but it is legend believed in as history never consciously invented, and growing out of certain

8

spots of the earth's surface, and supported by and drawing its life from the soil like a natural growth.

Such are the early Irish tales that cling around the mounds and cromlechs as that by which they are sustained, which was originally their source, and sustained them afterwards in a strong enduring life. It is evident that these cannot be classed with stories that float vaguely in an ideal world, which may happen in one place as well as another, and in which the names might be disarrayed without changing the character and consistency of the tale, and its relations, in time or otherwise, with other tales.

Foreigners are surprised to find the Irish claim for their own country an antiquity and a history prior to that of the neighbouring countries. Herein lie the proof and the explanation. The traditions and history of the mound-raising period have in other countries passed away. Foreign conquest, or less intrinsic force of imagination, and pious sentiment have suffered them to fall into oblivion; but in Ireland they have been all preserved in their original fulness and vigour, hardly a hue has faded, hardly a minute circumstance or articulation been suffered to decay.

The enthusiasm with which the Irish intellect seized upon the grand moral life of Christianity, and ideals so different from, and so hostile to, those of the heroic age, did not consume the traditions or destroy the pious and reverent spirit in which men still looked back upon those monuments of their own pagan teachers and kings, and the deep spirit of patriotism and affection with which the mind still clung to the old heroic age, whose types were warlike prowess, physical beauty, generosity, hospitality, love of family and nation, and all those noble attributes which constituted the heroic character as distinguished from the saintly. The Danish conquest, with its profound modification of Irish society, and consequent disruption of old habits and conditions of life, did not dissipate it; nor the more dangerous conquest of the Normans, with their own innate nobility of character, chivalrous daring, and continental grace and civilisation; nor the Elizabethan convulsions and systematic repression and destruction of all native phases of thought and feeling. Through all these storms, which successively assailed the heroic literature of ancient Ireland, it still held itself undestroyed. There were still found generous minds to shelter and shield the old tales and ballads, to feel the nobleness of that life of which they were the outcome, and to resolve that the soil of Ireland should not, so far as they had the power to prevent it, be denuded of its raiment of history and historic romance, or reduced again to primeval nakedness. The fruit of this persistency and unquenched love of country and its ancient traditions, is left to be enjoyed by us. There is not through the length and breadth of the country a conspicuous rath or barrow of which we cannot find the traditional history preserved in this ancient literature. The mounds of Tara, the great barrows along the shores of the Boyne, the raths of Slieve Mish, and Rathcrogan, and Teltown, the stone caiseals of Aran and Innishowen, and those that alone or in smaller groups stud the country over, are all, or nearly all, mentioned in this ancient literature, with the names and traditional histories of those over whom they were raised.

There is one thing to be learned from all this, which is, that we, at least, should not suffer these ancient monuments to be destroyed, whose history has been thus so astonishingly preserved. The English farmer may tear down the barrow which is unfortunate enough to be situated within his bounds. Neither he nor his neighbours know or can tell anything about its ancient history; the removed earth will help to make his cattle fatter and improve his crops, the stones will be useful to pave his roads and build his fences, and the savant can enjoy the rest; but the Irish farmer and landlord should not do or suffer this.

The instinctive reverence of the peasantry has hitherto been a great preservative; but the spread of education has to a considerable extent impaired this kindly sentiment, and the

10

progress of scientific farming, and the anxiety of the Royal Irish Academy to collect antiquarian trifles, have already led to the reckless destruction of too many. I think that no one who reads the first two volumes of this history would greatly care to bear a hand in the destruction of that tomb at Tara, in which long since his people laid the bones of Cuculain; and I think, too, that they would not like to destroy any other monument of the same age, when they know that the history of its occupant and its own name are preserved in the ancient literature, and that they may one day learn all that is to be known concerning it. I am sure that if the case were put fairly to the Irish landlords and country gentlemen, they would neither inflict nor permit this outrage upon the antiquities of their country. The Irish country gentleman prides himself on his love of trees, and entertains a very wholesome contempt for the mercantile boor who, on purchasing an old place, chops down the best timber for the market. And yet a tree, though cut down, may be replaced. One elm tree is as good as another, and the thinned wood, by proper treatment, will be as dense as ever; but the ancient mound, once carted away, can never be replaced any more. When the study of the Irish literary records is revived, as it certainly will be revived, the old history of each of these raths and cromlechs will be brought again into the light, and one new interest of a beautiful and edifying nature attached to the landscape, and affecting wholly for good the minds of our people.

Irishmen are often taunted with the fact that their history is yet unwritten, but that the Irish, as a nation, have been careless of their past is refuted by the facts which I have mentioned. A people who alone in Europe preserved, not in dry chronicles alone, but illuminated and adorned with all that fancy could suggest in ballad, and tale, and rude epic, the history of the mound-raising period, are not justly liable to this taunt. Until very modern times, history was the one absorbing pursuit of the Irish secular intellect, the delight of the noble, and the solace of the vile.

At present, indeed, the apathy on this subject is, I believe, without parallel in the world. It would seem as if the Irish, extreme in all things, at one time thought of nothing but their history, and, at another, thought of everything but it. Unlike those who write on other subjects, the author of a work on Irish history has to labour simultaneously at a two-fold task—he has to create the interest to which he intends to address himself.

The pre-Christian period of Irish history presents difficulties from which the corresponding period in the histories of other countries is free. The surrounding nations escape the difficulty by having nothing to record. The Irish historian is immersed in perplexity on account of the mass of material ready to his hand. The English have lost utterly all record of those centuries before which the Irish historian stands with dismay and hesitation, not through deficiency of materials, but through their excess. Had nought but the chronicles been preserved the task would have been simple. We would then have had merely to determine approximately the date of the introduction of letters, and allowing a margin on account of the bardic system and the commission of family and national history to the keeping of rhymed and alliterated verse, fix upon some reasonable point, and set down in order, the old successions of kings and the battles and other remarkable events. But in Irish history there remains, demanding treatment, that other immense mass of literature of an imaginative nature, illuminating with anecdote and tale the events and personages mentioned simply and without comment by the chronicler. It is this poetic literature which constitutes the stumbling-block, as it constitutes also the glory, of early Irish history, for it cannot be rejected and it cannot be retained. It cannot be rejected, because it contains historical matter which is consonant with and illuminates the dry lists of the chronologist, and it cannot be retained, for popular poetry is not history; and the task of distinguishing In such literature the fact from the fiction—where there is certainly fact and certainly fiction—is one of the most difficult to which the intellect can apply itself. That this difficulty has not been hitherto surmounted by Irish writers is no just reproach. For the last century, intellects of the highest attainments, trained and educated to the last degree, have been vainly endeavouring to solve a similar question in the far less copious and less varied heroic literature of Greece. Yet the labours of Wolfe, Grote, Mahaffy, Geddes, and Gladstone, have not been sufficient to set at rest the small question, whether it was one man or two or many who composed the Iliad and Odyssey, while the reality of the achievements of Achilles and even his existence might be denied or asserted by a scholar without general reproach. When this is the case with regard to the great heroes of the Iliad, I fancy it will be some time before the same problem will have been solved for the minor characters, and as it affects Thersites, or that eminent artist who dwelt at home in Hyla, being by far the most excellent of leather cutters. When, therefore, Greek still meets Greek in an interminable and apparently bloodless contest over the disputed body of the Iliad, and still no end appears, surely it would be madness for any one to sit down and gaily distinguish true from false in the immense and complex mass of the Irish bardic literature, having in his ears this century-lasting struggle over a single Greek poem and a single small phase of the pre-historic life of Hellas.

In the Irish heroic literature, the presence or absence of the marvellous supplies *no test whatsoever* as to the general truth or falsehood of the tale in which they appear. The marvellous is supplied with greater abundance in the account of the battle of Clontarf, and the wars of the O'Briens with the Normans, than in the tale in which is described the foundation of Emain Macha by Kimbay. Exact-thinking, scientific France has not hesitated to paint the battles of Louis XIV. with similar hues; and England, though by no means fertile in angelic interpositions, delights to adorn the barren tracts of her more popular histories with apocryphal anecdotes.

How then should this heroic literature of Ireland be treated in connection with the history of the country? The true method would certainly be to print it exactly as it is without excision or condensation. Immense it is, and immense it must remain. No men living, and no men to live, will ever so exhaust the meaning of any single tale as to render its publication unnecessary for the study of others. The order adopted should be that which the bards themselves deter mined, any other would be premature, and I think no other will ever take its place. At the commencement should stand the passage from the Book of Invasions, describing the occupation of the isle by Queen Keasair and her companions, and along with it every discoverable tale or poem dealing with this event and those characters. After that, all that remains of the cycle of which Partholan was the protagonist. Thirdly, all that relates to Nemeth and his sons, their wars with curt Kical the bow-legged, and all that relates to the Fomoroh of the Nemedian epoch, then first moving dimly in the forefront of our history. After that, the great Fir-bolgic cycle, a cycle janus-faced, looking on one side to the mythological period and the wars of the gods, and on the other, to the heroic, and more particularly to the Ultonian cycle. In the next place, the immense mass of bardic literature which treats of the Irish gods who, having conquered the Fir-bolgs, like the Greek gods of the age of gold dwelt visibly in the island until the coming of the Clan Milith, out of Spain. In the sixth, the Milesian invasion, and every accessible statement concerning the sons and kindred of Milesius. In the seventh, the disconnected tales dealing with those local heroes whose history is not connected with the great cycles, but who in the *fasti* fill the spaces between the divine period and the heroic. In the eighth, the heroic cycles, the Ultonian, the Temairian, and the Fenian, and after these the historic tales that, without forming cycles, accompany the course of history down to the extinction of Irish independence, and the transference to aliens of all the great sources of authority in the island.

This great work when completed will be of that kind of which no other European nation can supply an example. Every public library in the world will find it necessary to procure a copy. The chronicles will then cease to be so closely and exclusively studied. Every history of ancient Ireland will consist of more or less intelligent comments upon and theories formed in connection with this great series—theories which, in general, will only be formed in order to be destroyed. What the present age demands upon the subject of antique Irish history—an exact and scientific treatment of the facts supplied by our native authorities—will be demanded for ever. It will never be supplied. The history of Ireland will be contained in this huge publication. In it the poet will find endless themes of song, the philosopher strange workings of the human mind, the archeologist a mass of information, marvellous in amount and quality, with regard to primitive ideas and habits of life, and the rationalist materials for framing a scientific history of Ireland, which will be acceptable in proportion to the readableness of his style, and the mode in which his views may harmonize with the prevailing humour and complexion of his contemporaries.

Such a work it is evident could not be effected by a single individual. It must be a public and national undertaking, carried out under the supervision of the Royal Irish Academy, at the expense of the country.

The publication of the Irish bardic remains in the way that I have mentioned, is the only true and valuable method of presenting the history of Ireland to the notice of the world. The mode which I have myself adopted, that other being out of the question, is open to many obvious objections; but in the existing state of the Irish mind on the subject, no other is possible to an individual writer. I desire to make this heroic period once again a portion of the imagination of the country, and its chief characters as familiar in the minds of our people as they once were. As mere history, and treated in the method in which history is generally written at the present day, a work dealing with the early Irish kings and heroes would certainly not secure an audience. Those who demand such a treatment forget that there is not in the country an interest on the subject to which to appeal. A work treating of early Irish kings, in the same way in which the historians of neighbouring countries treat of their own early kings, would be, to the Irish public generally, unreadable. It might enjoy the reputation of being well written, and as such receive an honourable place in half-a-dozen public libraries, but it would be otherwise left severely alone. It would never make its way through that frozen zone which, on this subject, surrounds the Irish mind.

On the other hand, Irishmen are as ready as others to feel an interest in a human character, having themselves the ordinary instincts, passions, and curiosities of human nature. If I can awake an interest in the career of even a single ancient Irish king, I shall establish a train of thoughts, which will advance easily from thence to the state of society in which he lived, and the kings and heroes who surrounded, preceded, or followed him. Attention and interest once fully aroused, concerning even one feature of this landscape of ancient history, could be easily widened and extended in its scope.

Now, if nothing remained of early Irish history save the dry *fasti* of the chronicles and the Brehon laws, this would, I think, be a perfectly legitimate object of ambition, and would be consonant with my ideal of what the perfect flower of historical literature should be, to illuminate a tale embodying the former by hues derived from the Senchus Mor.

But in Irish literature there has been preserved, along with the *fasti* and the laws, this immense mass of ancient ballad, tale, and epic, whose origin is lost in the mists of extreme antiquity, and in which have been preserved the characters, relationships, adventures, and achievements of the vast majority of the personages whose names, in a gaunt nakedness, fill the books of the chroniclers. Around each of the greater heroes there groups itself a mass of bardic literature, varying in tone and statement, but preserving a substantial unity as to the general character and the more important achievements of the hero, and also, a fact upon which their general historical accuracy may be based with confidence, exhibiting a knowledge of that same prior and subsequent history recorded in the *fasti*. The literature which groups itself around a hero exhibits not only an unity with itself, but an acquaintance with the general course of the history of the country, and with preceding and succeeding kings.

The students of Irish literature do not require to be told this; for those who are not, I would give a single instance as an illustration.

In the battle of Gabra, fought in the third century, and in which Oscar, perhaps the greatest of all the Irish heroes heading the Fianna Eireen, contended against Cairbry of the Liffey, King of Ireland, and his troops, Cairbry on his side announces to his warriors that he would rather perish in this battle than suffer one of the Fianna to survive; but while he spoke—

> "Barran suddenly exclaimed—
> 'Remember Mall Mucreema, remember Art.
>
> "'Our ancestors fell there
>   By force of the treachery of the Fians;
>   Remember the hard tributes,
>   Remember the extraordinary pride.'"

Here the poet, singing only of the events of the battle of Gabra, shows that he was well-acquainted with all the relations subsisting for a long time between the Fians and the Royal family. The battle of Mucreema was fought by Cairbry's grandfather, Art, against Lewy Mac Conn and the Fianna Eireen.

Again, in the tale of the battle of Moy Leana, in which Conn of the Hundred Battles, the father of this same Art, is the principal character, the author of the tale mentions many times circumstances relating to his father, Felimy Rectmar, and his grandfather, Tuhall Tectmar. Such is the whole of the Irish literature, not vague, nebulous, and shifting, but following the course of the *fasti*, and regulated and determined by them. This argument has been used by Mr. Gladstone with great confidence, in order to show the substantial historical truthfulness of the Iliad, and that it is in fact a portion of a continuous historic sequence.

Now this being admitted, that the course of Irish history, as laid down by the chroniclers, was familiar to the authors of the tales and heroic ballads, one of two things must be admitted, either that the events and kings did succeed one another in the order mentioned by the chroniclers, or that what the chroniclers laid down was then taken as the theme of song by the bards, and illuminated and adorned according to their wont.

The second of these suppositions is one which I think few will adopt. Can we believe it possible that the bards, who actually supported themselves by the amount of pleasure which they gave their audiences, would have forsaken those subjects which were already popular, and those kings and heroes whose splendour and achievements must have affected, profoundly, the popular imagination, in order to invent stories to illuminate fabricated names. The thing is quite impossible. A practice which we can trace to the edge of that period whose historical character may be proved to demonstration, we may conclude to have extended on into the period immediately preceding that. When bards illuminated with stories and marvellous circumstances the battle of Clontarf and the battle of Moyrath, we may believe their predecessors to have done the same for the earlier centuries. The absence of an imaginative literature other than historical shows also that the literature must have followed, regularly, the course of the history, and was not an archaeological attempt to create an interest in names and events which were found in the chronicles.

It is, therefore, a reasonable conclusion that the bardic literature, where it reveals a clear sequence in the order of events, and where there is no antecedent improbability, supplies a trustworthy guide to the general course of our history.

So far as the clear light of history reaches, so far may these tales be proved to be historical. It is, therefore, reasonable to suppose that the same consonance between them and the actual course of events which subsisted during the period which lies in clear light, marked also that other preceding period of which the light is no longer dry.

The earliest manuscript of these tales is the Leabhar [1] na Huidhré, a work of the eleventh century, so that we may feel sure that we have them in a condition unimpaired by the revival of learning, or any archaeological restoration or improvement. Now, of some of these there have been preserved copies in other later MSS., which differ very little from the copies preserved in the Leabhar na Huidhré, from which we may conclude that these tales had arrived at a fixed state, and a point at which it was considered wrong to interfere with the text.

The feast of Bricrind is one of the tales preserved in this manuscript. The author of the tale in its present form, whenever he lived, composed it, having before him original books which he collated, using his judgment at times upon the materials to his hand. At one stage he observes that the books are at variance on a certain point, namely, that at which Cuculain, Conal the Victorious, and Laery Buada go to the lake of Uath in order to be judged by him. Some of the books, according to the author, stated that on this occasion the two latter behaved unfairly, but he agreed with those books which did not state this.

---

[1] Leabar na Heera.

We have, therefore, a tale penned in the eleventh century, composed at some time prior to this, and itself collected, not from oral tradition, but from books. These considerations would, therefore, render it extremely probable that the tales of the Ultonian period, with which the Leabhar na Huidhré is principally concerned, were committed to writing at a very early period.

To strengthen still further the general historic credibility of these tales, and to show how close to the events and heroes described must have been the bards who originally composed them, I would urge the following considerations.

With the advent of Christianity the mound-raising period passed away. The Irish heroic tales have their source in, and draw their interest from, the mounds and those laid in them. It would, therefore, be extremely improbable that the bards of the Christian period, when the days of rath and cairn had departed, would modify, to any considerable extent, the literature produced in conditions of society which had passed away.

Again, with the advent of Christianity, and the hold which the new faith took upon the finest and boldest minds in the country, it is plain that the golden age of bardic composition ended. The loss to the bards was direct, by the withdrawal of so much intellect from their ranks, and indirect, by the general substitution of other ideas for those whose ministers they themselves were. It is, therefore, probable that the age of production and creation, with regard to the ethnic history, ceased about the fifth and sixth centuries, and that, about that time, men began to gather up into a collected form the floating literature connected with the pagan period. The general current of mediaeval opinion attributes the collection of tales and ballads now known as the Tân-Bo-Cooalney to St. Ciaran, the great founder of the monastery of Clonmacnoise.

But if this be the case, we are enabled to take another step in the history of this most valuable literature. The tales of the Leabhar na Huidhré are in prose, but prose whose source and original is poetry. The author, from time to time, as if quoting an authority, breaks out with verse; and I think there is no Irish tale in existence without these rudimentary traces of a prior metrical cycle. The style and language are quite different, and indicate two distinct epochs. The prose tale is founded upon a metrical original, and composed in the meretricious style then in fashion, while the old metrical excerpts are pure and simple. This is sufficient, in a country like Ireland in those primitive times, to necessitate a considerable step into the past, if we desire to get at the originals upon which the prose tales were founded.

For in ancient Ireland the conservatism of the people was very great. It is the case in all primitive societies. Individual, initiative, personal enterprise are content to work within a very small sphere. In agriculture, laws, customs, and modes of literary composition, primitive and simple societies are very adverse to change.

When we see how closely the Christian compilers followed the early authorities, we can well believe that in the ethnic times no mind would have been sufficiently daring or sacrilegious to alter or pervert those epics which were in their eyes at the same time true and sacred.

In the perusal of the Irish literature, we see that the strength of this conservative instinct has been of the greatest service in the preservation of the early monuments in their purity. So much is this the case, that in many tales the most flagrant contradictions appear, the author or scribe being unwilling to depart at all from that which he found handed down. For instance, in the "Great Breach of Murthemney," we find Laeg at one moment killed, and in the next riding black Shanglan off the field. From this conservatism and careful following of authority, and the *littera scripta*, or word once spoken, I conclude that the distance in time between the prose tale and the metrical originals was very great, and, unless under such exceptional circumstances as the revolution caused by the introduction of Christianity, could not have been brought about within hundreds of years. Moreover, this same conservatism would have caused the tales concerning heroes to grow very slowly once they were actually formed. All the noteworthy events of the hero's life and his characteristics must have formed the original of the tales concerning him, which would have been composed during his life, or not long after his death.

I have not met a single tale, whether in verse or prose, in which it is not clearly seen that the author was not following authorities before him. Such traces of invention or decoration as may be met with are not suffered to interfere with the conduct of the tale and the statement of facts. They fill empty niches and adorn vacant places. For instance, if a king is represented as crossing the sea, we find that the causes leading to this, the place whence he set out, his companions, &c., are derived from the authorities, but the bard, at the same time, permits himself to give what seems to him to be an eloquent or beautiful description of the sea, and the appearance presented by the many-oared galleys. And yet the last transcription or recension of the majority of the tales was effected in Christian times, and in an age characterised by considerable classical attainments—a time when the imagination might have been expected to shake itself loose from old restraints, and freely invent. *A fortiori*, the more ancient bards, those of the ruder ethnic times, would have clung still closer to authority, deriving all their imaginative representations from preceding minstrels. There was no conscious invention at any time. Each cycle and tale grew from historic roots, and was developed from actual fact. So much may indeed be said for the more ancient tales, but the Ultonian cycle deals with events well within the historic period.

The era of Concobar Mac Nessa and the Red Branch knights of Ulster was long subsequent to the floruerunt of the Irish gods and their Titan-like opponents of this latter period, the names alone can be fairly held to be historic. What swells out the Irish chronicles to such portentous dimensions is the history of the gods and giants rationalised by mediaeval historians. Unable to ignore or excide what filled so much of the imagination of the country, and unable, as Christians, to believe in the divinity of the Tuátha De Danan and their predecessors, they rationalised all the pre-Milesian record. But the disappearance of the gods does not yet bring us within the penumbra of history. After the death of the sons of Milesius we find a long roll of kings. These were all topical heroes, founders of nations, and believed, by the tribes and tribal confederacies which they founded, to have been in their day the chief kings of Ireland. The point fixed upon by the accurate and sceptical Tiherna as the starting-point of trustworthy Irish history, was one long subsequent to the floruerunt of the gods; and the age of Concobar Mac Nessa and his knights was more than two centuries later than that of Kimbay and the foundation of Emain Macha. The floruit of Cuculain, therefore, falls completely within the historical penumbra, and the more carefully the enormous, and in the main mutually consistent and self-supporting, historical remains dealing with this period are studied, the more will this be believed. The minuteness, accuracy, extent, and verisimilitude of the literature, chronicles, pedigrees, &c., relating to this period, will cause the student to wonder more and more as he examines and collates, seeing the marvellous self-consistency and consentaneity of such a mass of varied recorded matter. The age, indeed, breathes sublimity, and abounds with the marvellous, the romantic, and the grotesque. But as I have already stated, the presence or absence of these qualities has no crucial significance. Love and reverence and the poetic imagination always effect such changes in the object of their passion. They are the essential condition of the transference of the real into the world of art. AEval, of Carriglea, the fairy queen of Munster, is one of the most important characters in the history of the battle of Clontarf, the character of which, and of the events that preceded and followed its occurrence, and the chieftains and warriors who fought on one side and the other, are identical, whether described by the bard singing, or by the monkish chronicler jotting down in plain prose the fasti for the year. The reader of these volumes can make such deductions as he pleases, on this account, from the bardic history of the Red Branch, and clip the wings of the tale, so that it may with him travel pedestrian. I know there are others, like myself, who will not hesitate for once to let the fancy roam and luxuriate in the larger spaces and freer airs of ancient song, nor fear that their sanity will be imperilled by the shouting of semi-divine heroes, and the sight of Cuculain entering battles with the Tuátha De Danan around him.

I hope on some future occasion to examine more minutely the character and place in literature of the Irish bardic remains, and put forward here these general considerations, from which the reader may presume that the Ultonian cycle, dealing as it does with Cuculain and his contemporaries, is in the main true to the facts of the time, and that his history, and that of the other heroes who figure in these volumes, is, on the whole, and omitting the marvellous, sufficiently reliable. I would ask the reader, who may be inclined to think that the principal character is too chivalrous and refined for the age, to peruse for himself the tale named the "Great Breach of Murthemney." He will there, and in many other tales and poems besides, see that the noble and pathetic interest which attaches to his character is substantially the same as I have represented in these volumes. But unless the student has read the whole of the Ultonian cycle, he should be cautious in condemning a departure in my work from any particular version of an event which he may have himself met. Of many minor events there are more than one version, and many scenes and assertions which he may think of importance would yet, by being related, cause inconsistency and contradiction. Of the nature of the work in which all should be introduced I have already given my opinion.

For the rest, I have related one or two great events in the life of Cuculain in such a way as to give a description as clear and correct as possible of his own character and history as related by the bards, of those celebrated men and women who were his contemporaries and of his relations with them, of the gods and supernatural powers in whom the people then believed, and of the state of civilisation which then prevailed. If I have done my task well, the reader will have been supplied, without any intensity of application on his part—a condition of the public mind upon which no historian of this country should count—with some knowledge of ancient Irish history, and with an interest in the subject which may lead him to peruse for himself that ancient literature, and to read works of a more strictly scientific nature upon the subject than those which I have yet written. But until such an interest is aroused, it is useless to swell the mass of valuable critical matter, which everyone at present is very well content to leave unread.

In the first volume, however, I have committed this error, that I did not permit it to be seen with sufficient clearness that the characters and chief events of the tale are absolutely historic; and that much of the colouring, inasmuch as its source must have been the centuries immediately succeeding the floruerunt of those characters, is also reliable as history, while the remainder is true to the times and the state of society which then obtained. The story seems to progress too much in the air, too little in time and space, and seems to be more of the nature of legend and romance than of actual historic fact seen through an imaginative medium. Such is the history of Concobar Mac Nessa and his knights—historic fact seen through the eyes of a loving wonder.

Indeed, I must confess that the blaze of bardic light which illuminates those centuries at first so dazzled the eye and disturbed the judgment, that I saw only the literature, only the epic and dramatic interest, and did not see as I should the distinctly historical character of the age around which that literature revolves, wrongly deeming that a literature so noble, and dealing with events so remote, must have originated mainly or altogether in the imagination. All the borders of the epic representation at which, in the first volume, I have aimed, seem to melt, and wander away vaguely on every side into space and time. I have now taken care to remedy that defect, supplying to the unset picture the clear historical frame to which it is entitled. I will also request the reader, when the two volumes may diverge in tone or statement, to attach greater importance to the second, as the result of wider and more careful reading and more matured reflection.

A great English poet, himself a severe student, pronounced the early history of his own country to be a mere scuffling of kites and crows, as indeed are all wars which lack the sacred bard, and the sacred bard is absent where the kites and crows pick out his eyes. That the Irish kings and heroes should succeed one another, surrounded by a blaze of bardic light, in which both themselves and all those who were contemporaneous with them are seen clearly and distinctly, was natural in a country where in each little realm or sub-kingdom the ard-ollav was equal in dignity to the king, which is proved by the equivalence of their cries. The dawn of English history is in the seventh century—a late dawn, dark and sombre, without a ray of cheerful sunshine; that of Ireland dates reliably from a point before the commencement of the Christian era luminous with that light which never was on sea or land—thronged with heroic forms of men and women—terrible with the presence of the supernatural and its over-arching power.

Educated Irishmen are ignorant of, and indifferent to, their history; yet from the hold of that history they cannot shake themselves free. It still haunts the imagination, like Mordecai at Haman's gate, a cause of continual annoyance and vexation. An Irishman can no more release himself from his history than he can absolve himself from social and domestic duties. He may outrage

26

it, but he cannot placidly ignore. Hence the uneasy, impatient feeling with which the subject is generally regarded.

I think that I do not exaggerate when I say that the majority of educated Irishmen would feel grateful to the man who informed them that the history of their country was valueless and unworthy of study, that the pre-Christian history was a myth, the post-Christian mere annals, the mediaeval a scuffling of kites and crows, and the modern alone deserving of some slight consideration. That writer will be in Ireland most praised who sets latest the commencement of our history. Without study he will be pronounced sober and rational before the critic opens the book. So anxious is the Irish mind to see that effaced which it is conscious of having neglected.

There are two compositions which affect an interest comparable to that which Ireland claims for her bardic literature, One is the Ossian of MacPherson, the other the Nibelungen Lied.

If we are to suppose Macpherson faithfully to have written down, printed, and published the floating disconnected poems which he found lingering in the Scotch highlands, how small, comparatively, would be their value as indications of antique thought and feeling, reduced then for the first time to writing, sixteen hundred years after the time of Ossian and his heroes, in a country not the home of those heroes, and destitute of the regular bardic organisation. The Ossianic tales and poems still told and sung by the Irish peasantry at the present day in the country of Ossian and Oscar, would be, if collected even now, quite as valuable, if not more so. Truer to the antique these latter are, for in them the cycles are not blended. The Red Branch heroes are not confused with Ossian's Fianna.

But MacPherson's Ossian is not a translation. In the publications of the Irish Ossianic poetry we see what that poetry really was—

rude, homely, plain-spoken, leagues removed from the nebulous sublimity of MacPherson.

With regard to the other, the Germans, who naturally desire to refer its composition to as remote a date as possible, and who arguing from no scientific data, but only style, ascribe the authorship of the Nibelungen to a poet living in the latter part of the twelfth century. Be it remembered, that the poem does not purport to be a collection of the scattered fragments of a cycle, but an original composition, then actually imagined and written. It does not even purport to deal with the ethnic times. *Its heroes are Christian heroes. They attend Mass.* The poem is not true, even to the leading features of the late period of history in which it is placed, if it have any habitat in the world of history at all. Attila, who died A.D. 450, and Theodoric, who did not die until the succeeding century, meet as coevals.

Turn we now from the sole boast of Germany to one out of a hundred in the Irish bardic literature. The Tân-bo-Cooalney was transcribed into the Leabhar na Huidhré in the eleventh century a manuscript whose date has been established by the consentaneity of Irish, French, and German scholarship. Mark, it was transcribed, not composed. The scribe records the fact:—

"Ego qui scripsi hanc historian aut vero fabulam, quibusdam fidem in hac historiâ aut fabulâ non commodo."

The Tân-bo-Cooalney was therefore *transcribed* by an ancient penman to the parchment of a still existing manuscript, in the century before that in which the German epic is presumed, from style only, and in the opinion of Germans, to have been *composed.*

The same scribe adds this comment with regard to its contents:—

"Qaedam autem poetica figmenta, quaedam ad delectationem stultorum."

28

Such scorn could not have been felt by one living in an age of bardic production. That independence and originality of thought, which caused Milton to despise the poets of the Restoration, are impossible in the simple stages of civilisation. The scribe who appended this very interesting comment to the subject of his own handiwork must have been removed by centuries from the date of its compilation. That the tale was, in his time, an ancient one, is therefore rendered extremely probable, the scribe himself indicating how completely out of sympathy he is with this form of literature, its antiquity and peculiar archaeological interest being, doubtless, the cause of the transcription.

Again, a close study of its contents, as of the contents of all the Irish historic tales, proves that in its present form, whenever that form was superadded, it is but a representation in prose of a pre-existing metrical original. Under this head I have already made some remarks, which, I shall request the reader to re-peruse

Once more, it deals with a particular event in Irish history, and with distinct and definite kings, heroes, and bards, who flourished in the epoch of which it treats. In the synchronisms of Tiherna, in the metrical chronology of Flann, in all the various historical compositions produced in various parts of the country, the main features and leading characters of the Tân-bo-Cooalney suffer no material change, while the minor divergencies show that the chronology of the annals and annalistic poems were not drawn from the tale, but owe their origin to other sources. Moreover, this epic is but a portion of the great Ultonian or Red Branch cycle, all the parts of which pre-suppose and support one another; and that cycle is itself a portion of the history of Ireland, and pre-supposes other preceding and succeeding cyles, preceding and succeeding kings. The event of which this epic treats occurred at the time of the Incarnation, and its characters are the leading Irish kings and warriors of that date. Such is the Tân-bo-Cooalney.

This being so, how have the English literary classes recognised, or how treated, our claim to the possession of an antique literature of peculiar historical interest, and by reason of that antiquity, a matter of concern to all Aryan nations? The conquest has not more constituted the English Parliament guardian and trustee of Ireland, for purposes of legislation and government, than it has vested the welfare and fame of our literature and antiquities in the hands of English scholarship. London is the headquarters of the intellectualism and of the literary and historical culture of the Empire. It is the sole dispenser of fame. It alone influences the mind of the country and guides thought and sentiment. It can make and mar reputations. What it scorns or ignores, the world, too, ignores and scorns. How then has the native literature of Ireland been treated by the representatives of English scholarship and literary culture? Mr. Carlyle is the first man of letters of the day, his the highest name as a critic upon, and historian of, the past life of Europe. Let us hear him upon this subject, admittedly of European importance.

Miscellaneous Essays, Vol. III., page 136. "Not only as the oldest Tradition of Modern Europe does it—the Nibelungen—possess a high antiquarian interest, but farther, and even in the shape we now see it under, unless the epics of the son of Fingal had some sort of authenticity, it is our oldest poem also."

Poor Ireland, with her hundred ancient epics, standing at the door of the temple of fame, or, indeed, quite behind the vestibule out of the way! To see the Swabian enter in, crowned, to a flourish of somewhat barbarous music, was indeed bad enough, but Mr. MacPherson!

They manage these things rather better in France, *vide passim* "La Révue Celtique."

Of the literary value of the bardic literature I fear to write at all, lest I should not know how to make an end. Rude indeed it is, but great. Like the central chamber of that huge tumulus[2] on the Boyne, overarched with massive unhewn rocks, its very ruggedness strikes an awe which the orderly arrangement of smaller and more reasonable thoughts, cut smooth by instruments inherited from classic times, fails so often to inspire. The labour of the Attic chisel may be seen since its invention in every other literary workshop of Europe, and seen in every other laboratory of thought the transmitted divine fire of the Hebrew. The bardic literature of Erin stands alone, as distinctively and genuinely Irish as the race itself, or the natural aspects of the island. Rude indeed it is, but like the hills which its authors tenanted with gods, holding dells[3] of the most perfect beauty, springs of the most touching pathos. On page 33, Vol. I., will be seen a poem [4] by Fionn upon the spring-time, made, as the old unknown historian says, to prove his poetic powers—a poem whose antique language relegates it to a period long prior to the tales of the Leabhar na Huidhré, one which, if we were to meet side by side with the "Ode to Night," by Alcman, in the Greek anthology, we would not be surprised; or those lines on page 203, Vol. I., the song of Cuculain, forsaken by his people, watching the frontier of his country—

"Alone in defence of the Ultonians,
 Solitary keeping ward over the province"

or the death[5] of Oscar, on pages 34 and 35, Vol. I., an excerpt condensed from the Battle of Gabra. Innumerable such tender and thrilling passages.

To all great nations their history presents itself under the aspect of poetry; a drama exciting pity and terror; an epic with unbroken continuity, and a wide range of thought, when the intellect is

---

[2] New Grange anciently Cnobgha, and now also Knowth.
[3] Those sacred hills will generally be found to have this character
[4] Publications of Ossianic Society, page 303, Vol. IV.
[5] Publications of Ossianic Society, Vol. I.

satisfied with coherence and unity, and the imagination by extent and diversity. Such is the bardic history of Ireland, but with this literary defect. A perfect epic is only possible when the critical spirit begins to be in the ascendant, for with the critical spirit comes that distrust and apathy towards the spontaneous literature of early times, which permit some great poet so to shape and alter the old materials as to construct a harmonious and internally consistent tale, observing throughout a sense of proportion and a due relation of the parts. Such a clipping and alteration of the authorities would have seemed sacrilege to earlier bards. In mediaeval Ireland there was, indeed, a subtle spirit of criticism; but under its influence, being as it was of scholastic origin, no great singing men appeared, re-fashioning the old rude epics; and yet, the very shortcomings of the Irish tales, from a literary point of view, increase their importance from a historical. Of poetry, as distinguised from metrical composition, these ancient bards knew little. The bardic literature, profoundly poetic though it be, in the eyes of our ancestors was history, and never was anything else. As history it was originally composed, and as history bound in the chains of metre, that it might not be lost or dissipated passing through the minds of men, and as history it was translated into prose and committed to parchment. Accordingly, no tale is without its defects as poetry, possessing therefore necessarily, a corresponding value as history. But that there was in the country, in very early times, a high and rare poetic culture of the lyric kind, native in its character, ethnic in origin, unaffected by scholastic culture which, as we know, took a different direction; that one exquisite poem, in which the father of Ossian praises the beauty of the springtime in anapaestic [6] verse, would, even though it

---

[6] Cettemain | cain ree! | ro sair | an cuct | "He, Fionn MacCool, learned the three compositions which distinguish the poets, the TEINM LAEGHA, the IMUS OF OSNA, and the DICEDUE DICCENAIB, and it was then Fionn composed this poem to prove his poetry." In which of these three forms of metre the Ode to the spring-time is written I know not. Its form throughout is distinctly anapaestic.—S. O'G.

stood alone, both by the fact of its composition and the fact of its preservation, fully prove.

Much and careful study, indeed, it requires, if we would compel these ancient epics to yield up their greatness or their beauty, or even their logical coherence and imaginative unity—broken, scattered portions as they all are of that one enormous epic, the bardic history of Ireland. At the best we read without the key. The magic of the names is gone, or can only be partially recovered by the most tender and sympathetic study. Indeed, without reading all or many, we will not understand the superficial meaning of even one. For instance, in one of the many histories of Cuculain's many battles, we read this—

"It was said that Lu Mac AEthleen was assisting him."

This at first seems meaningless, the bard seeing no necessity for throwing further light on the subject; but, as we wander through the bardic literature, gradually the conception of this Lu grows upon the mind—the destroyer of the sons of Turann—the implacably filial—the expulsor of the Fomoroh—the source of all the sciences—the god of the Tuátha De Danan—the protector and guardian of Cuculain—Lu Lamfáda, son of Cian, son of Diancéct, son of Esric, son of Dela, son of Ned the war-god, whose tomb or temple, Aula Neid, may still be seen beside the Foyle. This enormous and seemingly chaotic mass of literature is found at all times to possess an inner harmony, a consistency and logical unity, to be apprehended only by careful study.

So read, the sublimity strikes through the rude representation. Astonished at himself, the student, who at first thinks that he has chanced upon a crowd of barbarians, ere long finds himself in the august presence of demi-gods and heroes.

A noble moral tone pervades the whole. Courage, affection, and truth are native to all who live in this world. Under the dramatic image of Ossian wrangling with the Talkend,[7] the bards, themselves vainly fighting against the Christian life, a hundred times repeat through the lips of Ossian like a refrain—

"We, the Fianna of Erin, never uttered falsehood,
    Lying was never attributed to us;
    By courage and the strength of our hands
    We used to come out of every difficulty."

Again: Fergus, the bard, inciting Oscar to his last battle—in that poem called the Rosc Catha of Oscar:—

"Place thy hand on thy gentle forehead
    Oscar, who never lied."[8]

And again, elsewhere in the Ossianic poetry:—

"Oscar, who never wronged bard or woman."

Strange to say, too, they inculcated chastity (see p. 257; vol. i.), an allusion taken from the "youthful adventures of Cuculain," Leabhar na Huidhré.

The following ancient rann contains the four qualifications of a bard:—

"Purity of hand, bright, without wounding,
    Purity of mouth, without poisonous satire,
    Purity of learning, without reproach,
    Purity, as a husband, in wedlock."

Moreover, through all this literature sounds a high clear note of chivalry, in this contrasting favourably with the Iliad, where no

---

[7] St. Patrick, on account of the tonsured crown.

[8] Publications of Ossianic Society, p. 159; vol. i.

man foregoes an advantage. Cuculain having slain the sons of Neara, "thought it unworthy of him to take possession of their chariot and horses." [9]Goll Mac Morna, in the Fenian or Ossianic cycle, declares to Conn Cedcathah[10] that from his youth up he never attacked an enemy by night or under any disadvantage, and many times we read of heroes preferring to die rather than outrage their geisa. [11]

A noble literature indeed it is, having too this strange interest, that though mainly characterised by a great plainness and simplicity of thought, and, in the earlier stages, of expression, we feel, oftentimes, a sudden weirdness, a strange glamour shoots across the poem when the tale seems to open for a moment into mysterious depths, druidic secrets veiled by time, unsunned caves of thought, indicating a still deeper range of feeling, a still lower and wider reach of imagination. A youth came once to the Fianna Eireen encamped at Locha Lein[12], leading a hound dazzling white, like snow. It was the same, the bard simply states, that was once a yew tree, flourishing fifty summers in the woods of Ioroway. Elsewhere, he is said to have been more terrible than the sun upon his flaming wheels. What meant this yew tree and the hound? Stray allusions I have met, but no history. The spirit of Coelté, visiting one far removed in time from the great captain of the Fianna, with a different name and different history, cries:—

"I was with thee, with Finn"—

giving no explanation.

To MacPherson, however, I will do this justice, that he had the merit to perceive, even in the debased and floating ballads of the highlands, traces of some past greatness and sublimity of thought,

---

[9] P. 155; vol. i.

[10] Conn of the hundred battles.

[11] Certain vows taken with their arms on being knighted.

[12] The Lakes of Killarney.

and to understand, he, for the first time, how much more they meant than what met the ear. But he saw, too, that the historical origin of the ballads, and the position in time and place of the heroes whom they praised, had been lost in that colony removed since the time of St. Columba from its old connection with the mother country. Thus released from the curb of history, he gave free rein to the imagination, and in the conventional literary language of sublimity, gave full expression to the feelings that arose within him, as to him, pondering over those ballads, their gigantesque element developed into a greatness and solemnity, and their vagueness and indeterminateness into that misty immensity and weird obscurity which, as constituent factors in a poem, not as back-ground, form one of the elements of the false sublime. Either not seeing the literary necessity of definiteness, or having no such abundant and ordered literature as we possess, upon which to draw for details, and being too conscientious to invent facts, however he might invent language, he published his epics of Ossian—false indeed to the original, but true to himself, and to the feelings excited by meditation upon them. This done, he had not sufficient courage to publish also the rude, homely, and often vulgar ballads—a step which, in that hard critical age, would have been to expose himself and his country to swift contempt. The thought of the great lexicographer riding rough-shod over the poor mountain songs which he loved, and the fame which he had already acquired, deterred and dissuaded him, if he had ever any such intention, until the opportunity was past.

MacPherson feared English public opinion, and fearing lied. He declared that to be a translation which was original work, thus relegating himself for ever to a dubious renown, and depriving his country of the honest fame of having preserved through centuries, by mere oral transmission, a portion, at least, of the antique Irish literature. To the magnanimity of his own heroes he could not attain:—

"Oscar, Oscar, who feared not armies—
Oscar, who never lied."

Of some such error as MacPherson's I have myself, with less excuse, been guilty, in chapters xi. and xii., Vol. I., where I attempt to give some conception of the character of the Ossianic cycle. The age and the heroes around whom that cycle revolves have, in the history of Ireland, a definite position in time; their battles, characters, several achievements, relationships, and pedigrees; their Dûns, and trysting-places, and tombs; their wives, musicians, and bards; their tributes, and sufferings, and triumphs; their internecine and other wars—are all fully and clearly described in the Ossianic cycle. They still remain demanding adequate treatment, when we arrive at the age of Conn, Art, and Cormac, kings of Tara in the second and third centuries of the Christian era. All have been forgotten for the sake of a vague representation of the more sublime aspects of the cycle, and the meretricious seductions of a form of composition easy to write and easy to read, and to which the unwary or unwise often award praise to which it has no claim.

On the other hand, chapter xi. purports only to be a representation of the feelings excited by this literature, and for every assertion there is authority in the cycle. Chapter xii., however, is a translation from the original. Every idea which it contains, except one, has been taken from different parts of the Ossianic poems, and all together expressthe graver attitude of the mind of Ossian towards the new faith. That idea, occurring in a separate paragraph in the middle of the page, though prevalent as a sentiment throughout all the conversations of Ossian with St. Patrick, has been, as it stands, taken from a meditation on life by St. Columbanus, one of the early Irish Saints—a meditation which, for subtle thought, for musical resigned sadness, tender brooding reflection, and exquisite Latin, is one of the masterpieces of mediaeval composition.

To the casual reader of the bardic literature the preservation of an ordered historical sequence, amidst that riotous wealth of imaginative energy, may appear an impossibility. Can we believe that forestine luxuriance not to have overgrown all highways, that flood of superabundant song not have submerged all landmarks? Be the cause what it may, the fact remains that they did not. The landmarks of history stand clear and fixed, each in its own place unremoved; and through that forest-growth the highways of history run on beneath over-arching, not interfering, boughs. The age of the predominance of Ulster does not clash with the age of the predominance of Tara; the Temairian kings are not mixed with the contemporary Fians. The chaos of the Nibelungen is not found here, nor the confusion of the Scotch ballads blending all the ages into one.

It is not imaginative strength that produces confusion, but imaginative weakness. The strong imagination which perceives definitely and realises vividly will not tolerate that obscurity so dear to all those who worship the eidola of the cave. Of each of these ages, the primary impressions were made in the bardic mind during the life-time of the heroes who gave to the epoch its character; and a strong impression made in such a mind could not have been easily dissipated or obscured. For it must be remembered, that the bardic literature of Ireland was committed to the custody of guardians whose character we ought not to forget. The bards were not the people, but a class. They were not so much a class as an organisation and fraternity acknowledging the authority of one elected chief. They were not loose wanderers, but a power in the State, having duties and privileges. The ard-ollav ranked next to the king, and his eric was kingly. Thus there was an educated body of public opinion entrusted with the preservation of the literature and history of the country, and capable of repressing the aberrations of individuals.

But the question arises, Did they so repress such perversions of history as their wandering undisciplined members might commit? Too much, of course, must not reasonably be expected. It was an age of creative thought, and such thought is difficult to control; but that one of the prime objects and prime works of the bards, as an organisation, was to preserve a record of a certain class of historical facts is certain. The succession of the kings and of the great princely families was one of these. The tribal system, with the necessity of affinity as a ground of citizenship, demanded such a preservation of pedigrees in every family, and particularly in the kingly houses. One of the chief objects of the triennial feis of Tara was the revision of such records by the general assembly of the bards, under the presidency of the Ard-Ollav of Ireland. In the more ancient times, such records were rhymed and alliterated, and committed to memory—a practice which, we may believe on the authority of Caesar, treating of the Gauls, continued long after the introduction of letters. Even at those local assemblies also, which corresponded to great central and national feis of Tara, the bards were accustomed to meet for that purpose. In a poem[13], descriptive of the fair[14] of Garman, we see this—

"Feasts with the great feasts of Temair,
Fairs with the fairs of Emania,
Annals there are verified."

In the existing literature we see two great divisions. On the one hand the epical, a realm of the most riotous activity of thought; on the other, the annalistic and genealogical, bald and bare to the last degree, a mere skeleton. They represent the two great hemispheres of the bardic mind, the latter controlling the former. Hence the orderly sequence of the cyclic literature; hence the strong confining banks between which the torrent of song rolls down through those centuries in which the bardic imagination reached its height. The consentaneity of the annals and the literature furnishes a trustworthy guide to the general course of history, until its guidance is barred by *a priori* considerations of a weightier nature, or by the statements of writers, having sources of information not open to us. For instance, the stream of Irish history must, for philosophical reasons, be no further traceable

---

[13] O'Curry's Manners and Customs, Vol. I., page 543.
[14] On the full meaning of this word "fair," see Chap. xiii., Vol. I.

than to that point at which it issues from the enchanted land of the Tuátha De Danan. At the limit at which the gods appear, men and history must disappear; while on the other hand, the statement of Tiherna, that the foundation of Emain Alacha by Kimbay is the first certain date in Irish history, renders it undesirable to attach more historical reality of characters, adorning the ages prior to B.C. 299, than we could to such characters as Romulus in Roman, or Theseus in Athenian history.

I desire here to record my complete and emphatic dissent from the opinions advanced by a writer in Hermathena on the subject of the Ogham inscriptions, and the introduction into this country of the art of writing. A cypher, i.e., an alphabet derived from a pre-existing alphabet, the Ogham may or may not have been. I advance no opinion upon that, but an invention of the Christian time it most assuredly was not. No sympathetic and careful student of the Irish bardic literature can possibly come to such a conclusion. The bardic poems relating to the heroes of the ethnic times are filled with allusions to Ogham inscriptions on stone, and contain some references to books of timber; but in my own reading I have not met with a single passage in that literature alluding to books of parchment and to rounded letters.

If the Ogham was derived from the Roman characters introduced by Christian missionaries, then these characters would be the more ancient, and Ogham the more modern; books and Roman characters would be the more poetical, and inscriptions on stone and timber in the Ogham characters the more prosaic. The bards relating the lives and deeds of the ancient heroes, would have ascribed to their times parchment books and the Roman characters, not stone and wood, and the Ogham.

In these compositions, whenever they were reduced to the form in which we find them to-day, the ethnic character of the times and the ethnic character of the heroes are clearly and universally observed. The ancient, the remote, the archaic clings to this literature. As Homer does not allude to writing, though all scholars agree that he lived in a lettered age, so the old bards do not allude to parchment and Roman characters, though the Irish epics, as distinguished from their component parts, reached their fixed state and their final development in times subsequent to the introduction of Christianity.

When and how a knowledge of letters reached this island we know not. From the analogy of Gaul, we may conclude that they were known for some time prior to their use by the bards. Caesar tells us that the Gaulish bards and druids did not employ letters for the preservation of their lore, but trusted to memory, assisted, doubtless, as in this country, by the mechanical and musical aid of verse. Whether the Ogham was a native alphabet or a derivative from another, it was at first employed only to a limited extent. Its chief use was to preserve the name of buried kings and heroes in the stone that was set above their tombs. It was, perhaps, invented, and certainly became fashionable on this account, straight strokes being more easily cut in stone than rounded or uncial characters. For the same reason it was generally employed by those who inscribed timber tablets, which formed the primitive book, ere they discovered or learned how to use pen, ink, and parchment. The use of Ogham was partially practised in the Christian period for sepultural purposes, being venerable and sacred from time. Hence the discovery of Ogham-inscribed stones in Christian cemeteries. On the other hand, the fact that the majority of these stones are discovered in raths and forts, i.e., the tombs of our Pagan ancestors, corroborates the fact implied in all the bardic literature, that the characters employed in the ethnic times were Oghamic, and affords another proof of the close conservative spirit of the bards in their transcription, compilation, or reformation of the old epics.

The full force of the concurrent authority of the bardic literature to the above effect can only be felt by one who has read that literature with care. He will find in all the epics no trace of original invention, but always a studied and conscientious following of authority. This being so, he will conclude that the universal ascription of Ogham, and Ogham only, to the ethnic times, arises solely from the fact that such was the alphabet then employed.

If letters were unknown in those times, the example of Homer shows how unlikely the later poets would have been to outrage so violently the whole spirit of the heroic literature. If rounded letters were then used, why the universal ascription of the late invented Ogham which, as we know from the cemeteries and other sources, was unpopular in the Christian age.

Cryptic, too, it was not. The very passages quoted in Hermathena to support this opinion, so far from doing so prove actually the reverse. When Cuculain came down into Meath on his first[15] foray, he found, on the lawn of the Dûn of the sons of Nectan, a pillar stone with this inscription in Ogham—"Let no one pass without an offer of a challenge of single combat." The inscription was, of course, intended for all to read. Should there be any bardic passage in which Ogham inscriptions are alluded to as if an obscure form of writing, the natural explanation is, that this kind of writing was passing or had passed into desuetude at the time that particular passage was composed; but I have never met with any such. The ancient bard, who, in the Tân-bo-Cooalney, describes the slaughter of Cailitin and his sons by Cuculain, states that there was an inscription to that effect, written in Ogham, upon the stone over their tomb, beginning thus—"Take notice"—evidently intended for all to read. The tomb, by the way, was a rath—again showing the ethnic character of the alphabet.

In the Annals of the Four Masters, at the date 1499 B.C., we read these words:—

---

[15] Vol. I., page 155.

"THE FLEET OF THE SONS OF MILITH CAME TO IRELAND TO TAKE IT FROM THE TUÁTHA DE DANAN," i.e., the gods of the ethnic Irish.

Without pausing to enquire into the reasonableness of the date, it will suffice now to state that at this point the bardic history of Ireland cleaves asunder into two great divisions—the mythological or divine on the one hand, and the historical or heroic-historical on the other. The first is an enchanted land—the world of the Tuátha De Danan—the country of the gods. There we see Mananan with his mountain-sundering sword, the Fraygarta; there Lu Lamfada, the deliverer, pondering over his mysteries; there Bove Derg and his fatal[16] swine-herd, Lir and his ill-starred children, Mac Mánar and his harp shedding death from its stricken wires, Angus Og, the beautiful, and he who was called the mighty father, Eochaidht[17] Mac Elathan, a land populous with those who had partaken of the feast of Goibneen, and whom, therefore, weapons could not slay, who had eaten [18] at the

---

[16] Every feast to which he came ended in blood. He was present at the death of Conairey Mor, Chap. xxxiii., Vol. I.

[17] Ay-o-chee, written Yeoha in Vol. I.

[18] In early Greek literature the province of history has been already separated from that of poetry. The ancient bardic lore and primaeval traditions were refined to suit the new and sensitive poetic taste. No commentator has been able to explain the nature of ambrosia. In the genuine bardic times, no such vague euphuism would have been tolerated as that of Homer on this subject. The nature of Olympian ambrosia would have been told in language as clear as that in which Homer describes the preparation of that Pramnian bowl for which Nestor and Machaon waited while Hecamede was grating over it the goat's milk cheese, or that in which the Irish bards described the ambrosia of the Tuátha De Danan, which, indeed, was no more poetic and awe-inspiring than plain bacon prepared by Mananan from his herd of enchanted pigs, living invisible like himself in the plains of Tir-na-n-Og, the land of the ever-young. On the other hand, there is a vagueness about the Feed Fia which would seem to indicate the growth of a more awe-stricken mood in describing things supernatural. The Faed Fia of the Greek gods has been refined by Homer into "much darkness," which, from an artistic point of view, one can hardly help imagining that Homer nodded as he wrote.

the table of Mananan, and would never grow old, who had invented for themselves the Faed Fia, and might not be seen of the gross eyes of men; there steeds like Anvarr crossing the wet sea like a firm plain; there ships whose rudder was the will, and whose sails and oars the wish, of those they bore[19]; there hounds like that one of Ioroway, and spears like fiery flying serpents. These are the Tuátha De Danan[20], fairy princes, Tuátha; gods, De; of Dana, Danan, otherwise Ana and the Moreega, or great queen; mater [21] deorum Hibernensium—"well she used to cherish [22] the gods." Limitless, this divine population, dwelling in all the seas and estuaries, river and lakes, mountains and fairy dells, in that enchanted Erin which was theirs.

But they have not started into existence suddenly, like the gods of Rome, nor is their genealogy confined to a single generation like those of Greece. Behind them extends a long line of ancestors, and a history reaching into the remotest depths of the past. As the Greek gods dethroned the Titans, so the Irish gods drove out or subjected the giants of the Fir-bolgs; but in the Irish mythology, we find both gods and giants descended from other ancient races of deities, called the Clanna Nemedh and the Fomoroh, and these a branch of a divine cycle; yet more ancient the race of Partholan, while Partholan himself is not the eldest.

The history of the Italian gods is completely lost. For all that the early Roman literature tells us of their origin, they may have been either self-created or eternal. Rome was a seedling shaken from some old perished civilisation. The Romans created their own

---

[19] Cf. The barks of the Phoenicians in the Odyssey.

[20] A mystery still hangs over this three-formed name. The full expression, Tuátha De Danan, is that generally employed, less frequently Tuátha De, and sometimes, but not often, Tuátha. Tuátha also means people. In mediaeval times the name lost its sublime meaning, and came to mean merely "fairy," no greater significance, indeed, attaching to the invisible people of the island after Christianity had destroyed their godhood.

[21] Cormac's Glossary

[22] Scholiast noting same Glossary.

44

empire, but they inherited their gods. They supply no example of an Aryan nation evolving its own mythology and religion. Regal Rome, as we know from Niebuhr, was not the root from which our Rome sprang, but an old imperial city, from whose ashes sprang that Rome we all know so well. The mythology of the Latin writers came to them full-grown.

The gods of Greece were a creation of the Greek mind, indeed; but of their ancestry, i.e., of their development from more ancient divine tribes, we know little. Like Pallas, they all but start into existence suddenly full-grown. Between the huge physical entities of the Greek theogonists and the Olympian gods, there intervenes but a single generation. For this loss of the Grecian mythology, and this substitution of Nox and Chaos for the remote ancestors of the Olympians, we have to thank the early Greek philosophers, and the general diffusion of a rude scientific knowledge, imparting a physical complexion to the mythological memory of the Greeks.

In the theogony of the ancient inhabitants of this country, we have an example of a slowly-growing, slowly-changing mythology, such as no other nation in the world can supply. The ancestry of the Irish gods is not bounded by a single generation or by twenty. The Tuátha De Danan of the ancient Irish are the final outcome and last development of a mythology which we can see advancing step by step, one divine tribe pushing out another, one family of gods swallowing up another, or perishing under the hands of time and change, to make room for another. From Angus Og, the god of youth and love and beauty, whose fit home was the woody slopes of the Boyne, where it winds around Rosnaree, we count fourteen generations to Nemedh and four to Partholan, and Partholan is not the earliest. As the bards recorded with a zeal and minuteness, so far as I can see, without parallel, the histories of the families to which they were adscript, so also they recorded with equal patience and care the far-extending pedigrees of those other families—invisible indeed, but to them more real and more awe-inspiring—who dwelt by the sacred lakes and rivers, and in the folds of the fairy hills, and the great raths and cairns reared for them by pious hands.

The extent, diversity, and populousness of the Irish mythological cycles, the history of the Irish gods, and the gradual growth of that mythology of which the Tuátha De Danan, i.e., the gods of the historic period, were the final development, can only be rightly apprehended by one who reads the bardic literature as it deals with this subject. That literature, however, so far from having been printed and published, has not even been translated, but still moulders in the public libraries of Europe, those who, like myself, are not professed Irish scholars, being obliged to collect their information piece-meal from quotations and allusions of those who have written upon the subject in the English or Latin language. For to read the originals aright needs many years of labour, the Irish tongue presenting at different epochs the characteristics of distinct languages, while the peculiarities of ancient caligraphy, in the defaced and illegible manuscripts, form of themselves quite a large department of study. Stated succinctly, the mythological record of the bards, with its chronological decorations, runs thus:—

AGE OF KEASAIR.

2379 B.C. the gods of the KEASAIRIAN cycle, Bith, Lara, and Fintann, and their wives, KEASAIR, Barran and Balba; their sacred places, Carn Keshra, Keasair's tomb or temple, on the banks of the Boyle, Ard Laran on the Wexford Coast, Fert Fintann on the shores of Lough Derg.

About the same time Lot Luaimenich, Lot of the Lower Shannon, an ancient sylvan deity.

AGE OF PARTHOLAN AND THE EARLIEST FOMORIAN GODS.

46

2057 B.C. a new spiritual dynasty, of which PARTHOLAN was father and king. Though their worship was extended over Ireland, which is shown by the many different places connected with their history, yet the hill of Tallaght, ten miles from Dublin, was where they were chiefly adored. Here to the present day are the mounds and barrows raised in honour of the deified heroes of this cycle, PARTHOLAN himself, his wife Delgna, his sons, Rury, Slaney, and Laighlinni, and among others, the father of Irish hospitality, bearing the expressive name of Beer. Now first appear the Fomoroh giant princes, under the leadership of curt Kical, son of Niul, son of Garf, son of U-Mor—a divine cycle intervening between KEASAIR and PARTHOLAN, but not of sufficient importance to secure a separate chapter and distinct place in the annals. Battles now between the Clan Partholan and the Fomoroh, on the plain of Ith, beside the river Finn, Co. Donegal, so called from Ith[23], son of Brogan, the most ancient of the heroes, slain here by the Tuátha De Danan, but more anciently known by some lost Fomorian name; also at Iorrus Domnan, now Erris, Co. Mayo, where Kical and his Fomorians first reached Ireland. These battles are a parable—objective representations of a fact in the mental history of the ancient Irish—typifying the invisible war waged between Partholanian and Fomorian deities for the spiritual sovereignty of the Gael.

AGE OF THE NEMEDIAN GODS AND SECOND CYCLE OF THE FOMORIANS.

1700 B.C. age of the NEMEDIAN divinities, a later branch of the PARTHOLANIAN *vide post* NEMEDIAN pedigree. NEMEDH, his wife Maca (first appearance of Macha, the war goddess, who gave her name to Armagh, i.e., Ard Macha, the Height of Macha), Iarbanel; Fergus, the Red-sided, and Starn, sons of Nemedh; Beothah, son of Iarbanel; Erglann, son of Beoan, son of Starn; Siméon Brac, son of Starn; Ibath, son of Beothach;

---

[23] See Vol. I, p. 60

Britan Mael, son of Fergus. This must be remembered, that not one of the almost countless names that figure in the Irish mythology is of fanciful origin. They all represent antique heroes and heroines, their names being preserved in connection with those monuments which were raised for purposes of sepulture or cult.

Wars now between the Clanna Nemedh and the second cycle of the Fomoroh, led this time by Faebar and More, sons of Dela, and Coning, son of Faebar; battles at Ros Freachan, now Rosreahan, barony of Murresk, Co. Mayo, at Slieve Blahma[24] and Murbolg, in Dalaradia (Murbolg, i.e., the stronghold of the giants,) also at Tor Coning, now Tory Island.

FIRBOLGS AND THIRD CYCLE OF THE FOMOROH.

1525 B.C. Age of the FIRBOLGS and third cycle of the Fomorians, once gods, but expulsed from their sovereignty by the Tuátha De Danan, after which they loom through the heroic literature as giants of the elder time, overthrown by the gods. From the FIRBOLGS were descended, or claimed to have descended, the Connaught warriors who fought with Queen Meave against Cuculain, also the Clan Humor, appearing in the Second Volume, also the heroes of Ossian, the Fianna Eireen. Even in the time of Keating, Irish families traced thither their pedigrees. The great chiefs of the FIR-BOLGIC dynasty were the five sons of Dela, Gann, Genann, Sengann, Rury, and Slaney, with their wives Fuad, Edain, Anust, Cnucha, and Libra; also their last and most potent king, EOCAIDH MAC ERC, son of Ragnal, son of Genann, whose tomb or temple may be seen to-day at Ballysadare, Co. Sligo, on the edge of the sea.

---

[24] Slieve Blahma, now Slieve Bloom, a mountain range famous in our mythology; one of the peaks, Ard Erin, sacred to Eiré, a goddess of the Tuátha De Danan, who has given her name to the island. The sites of all these mythological battles, where they are not placed in the haunted mountains, will be found to be a place of raths and cromlechs.

The Fomorians of this age were ruled over by Baler Beimenna and his wife Kethlenn. Their grandson was Lu Lamáda, one of the noblest of the Irish gods.

The last of the mythological cycles is that of the Tuátha De Danan, whose character, attributes, and history will, I hope, be rendered interesting and intelligible in my account of Cuculain and the Red Branch of Ulster.

Irish history has suffered from rationalism almost more than from neglect and ignorance. The conjectures of the present century are founded upon mediaeval attempts to reduce to verisimilitude and historical probability what was by its nature quite incapable of such treatment. The mythology of the Irish nation, being relieved of the marvellous and sublime, was set down with circumstantial dates as a portion of the country's history by the literary men of the middle ages. Unable to excide from the national narrative those mythological beings who filled so great a place in the imagination of the times, and unable, as Christians, to describe them in their true character as gods, or, as patriots, in the character which they believed them to possess, namely, demons, they rationalized the whole of the mythological period with names, dates, and ordered generations, putting men for gods, flesh and blood for that invisible might, till the page bristled with names and dates, thus formulating, as annals, what was really the theogony and mythology of their country. The error of the mediaeval historians is shared by the not wiser moderns. In the generations of the gods we seem to see prehistoric racial divisions and large branches of the Aryan family, an error which results from a neglect of the bardic literature, and a consequently misdirected study of the annals.

As history, the pre-Milesian record contains but a limited supply of objective truths; but as theogony, and the history of the Irish gods, these much abused chronicles are as true as the roll of the kings of England.

These divine nations, with their many successive generations and dynasties, constitute a single family; they are all inter-connected and spring from common sources, and where the literature permits us to see more clearly, the earlier races exhibit a common character. Like a human clan, the elements of this divine family grew and died, and shed forth seedlings which, in time, over-grew and killed the parent stock. Great names became obscure and passed away, and new ones grew and became great. Gods, worshipped by the whole nation, declined and became topical, and minor deities expanding, became national. Gods lost their immortality, and were remembered as giants of the old time—mighty men, which were of yore, men of renown.

"The gods which were of old time rest in their tombs,"

sang the Egyptians, consciously ascribing mortality even to gods. Such was Mac Ere, King of Fir-bolgs. His temple[25], beside the sea at Iorrus Domnan[26], became his tomb. Daily the salt tide embraces the feet of the great tumulus, regal amongst its smaller comrades, where the last king of Fir-bolgs was worshipped by his people. "Good[27] were the years of the sovereignty of Mac Ere. There was no wet or tempestuous weather in Ireland, nor was there any unfruitful year." Such were all the predecessors of the children of Dana—gods which were of old times, that rest in their tombs; and the days, too, of the Tuátha De Danan were numbered. They, too, smitten by a more celestial light, vanished from their hills, like Ossian lamenting over his own heroes; those others still mightier, might say:—

"Once every step which we took might be heard throughout the firmament. Now, all have gone, they have melted into the air."

---

[25] Strand near Ballysadare, Co. Sligo
[26] Keating—evidently quoting a bardic historian
[27] Temple—vide post.

But that divine tree, though it had its branches in fairy-land, had its roots in the soil of Erin. An unceasing translation of heroes into Tir-na-n-og went on through time, the fairy-world of the bards, receiving every century new inhabitants, whose humbler human origin being forgotten, were supplied there with both wives and children. The apotheosis of great men went forward, tirelessly; the hero of one epoch becoming the god of the next, until the formation of the Tuátha De Danan, who represent the gods of the historic ages. Had the advent of exact genealogy been delayed, and the creative imagination of the bards suffered to work on for a couple of centuries longer, unchecked by the historical conscience, Cuculain's human origin would, perhaps, have been forgotten, and he would have been numbered amongst the Tuátha De Danan, probably, as the son of Lu Lamfáda and the Moreega, his patron deities. It was, indeed, a favourite fancy of the bards that not Sualtam, but Lu Lamfáda himself, was his father; this, however, in a spiritual or supernatural sense, for his age was far removed from that of the Tuátha De Danan, and falling well within the scope of the historic period. Even as late as the time of Alexander, the Greeks could believe a great contemporary warrior to be of divine origin, and the son of Zeus.

When the Irish bards began to elaborate a general history of their country, they naturally commenced with the enumeration of the elder gods. I at one time suspected that the long pedigrees running between those several divisions of the mythological period were the invention of mediaeval historians, anxious to spin out the national record, that it might reach to Shinar and the dispersion. Not only, however, was such fabrication completely foreign to the genius of the literature, but in the fragments of those early divine cycles, we see that each of these personages was at one time the centre of a literature, and holds a definite place as regards those who went before and came after. These pedigrees, as I said before, have no historical meaning, being pre-Milesian, and therefore absolutely prehistoric; but as the genealogy of the gods, and as representing the successive generations of that invisible family, whose history not one or ten bards, but the whole bardic and druidic organisation of the island, delighted to record, collate, and verify—those pedigrees are as reliable as that of any of the regal clans. They represent accurately the mythological panorama, as it unrolled itself slowly through the centuries before the imagination and spirit of our ancestors accurately that divine drama, millennium—lasting, with its exits and entrances of gods. Millennium-lasting, and more so, for it is plain that one divine generation represents on the average a much greater space of time than a generation of mortal men. The former probably represents the period which would elapse before a hero would become so divine, that is, so consecrated in the imagination of the country, as to be received into the family of the gods. Cuculain died in the era of the Incarnation, three hundred years, if not more, before the country even began to be Christianised, yet he is never spoken of as anything but a great hero, from which one of two things would follow, either that the apotheosis of heroes needed the lapse of centuries, or that, during the first, second, third, and fourth centuries, the historical conscience was so enlightened, and a positive definite knowledge of the past so universal, that the translation of heroes into the divine clans could no longer take place. The latter is indeed the more correct view; but the reader will, I think, agree with me that the divine generations, taken generally, represent more than the average space of man's life. To what remote unimagined distances of time those earlier cycles extend has been shown by an examination of the tombs of the lower Moy Tura. The ancient heroes there interred were those who, as Fir-bolgs, preceded the reign of the Tuáth De Danan, coming long after the Clanna Nemedh in the divine cycle, who were themselves preceded by the children of Partholan, who were subsequent to the Queen Keasair. Such then being the position in the divine cycle of the Fir-bolgs, an examination of the Firbolgic raths on Moy Tura has revealed only implements of stone, proving demonstratively that the early divine cycles originated before the bronze age in Ireland, whenever that commenced. Those heroes who, as Fir-bolgs, received divine honours, lived in the age of stone. So far is it from being the case, that the mythological record has been extended and unduly stretched, to enable the monkish historians to connect the Irish pedigrees with those of the Mosaic record, that it has, I believe, been contracted for this purpose.

The reader will be now prepared to peruse with some interest and understanding one or two of the mythological pedigrees. To these I have at times appended the dates, as given in the chronicles, to show how the early historians rationalised the pre-historic record.

Angus Og, the Beautiful, represents the Greek Eros. He was surnamed Og, or young; Mac-an-Og, or the son of youth; Mac-an-Dagda, son of the Dagda. He was represented with a harp, and attended by bright birds, his own transformed kisses, at whose singing love arose in the hearts of youths and maidens. To him and to his father the great tumulus of New Grange, upon the Boyne, was sacred.

> "I visited the Royal Brugh that stands
> By the dark-rolling waters of the Boyne,
> Where Angus Og magnificently dwells."

He was the patron god of Diarmid, the Paris of Ossian's Fianna, and removed him into Tir-na-n-Og, when he died, having been ripped by the tusks of the wild boar on the peaks of Slieve Gulban.

Lu Lamfáda was the patron god of Cuculain. He was surnamed Ioldana, as the source of the sciences, and represented the Greek Apollo. The latter was argurgurotoxos[28], but Lu was a sling bearing god. Of Fomorian descent on the mother's side, he joined his father's people, the Tuátha De Danan, in the great war against the Fomoroh. He is principally celebrated for his oppression of the sons of Turann, in vengeance for the murder of his father.

---

[28] Greek in the original

53

ANGUS OG, (circa 1500 B.C.)

   son of

THE DAGDA, (Zeus)

   son of

Elathan,

   son of

Dela,

   son of

Ned,

   son of

Indaei,

LU LAMFADA, (circa 1500 B.C.)

   son of

Cian,

   son of

Diancéct, (god the healer)

   son of

Esric,

   son of

Dela

   son of

Ned,

   son of

Indaei,

   son of

ALLDAEI.

Amongst other Irish gods was Bove Derg, who dwelt invisible in the Galtee mountains, and in the hills above Lough Derg. The transformed children alluded to in Vol. I. were his grand-children. It was his goldsmith Len, who gave its ancient name to the Lakes of Killarney, Locha Lein. Here by the lake he worked, surrounded by rainbows and showers of fiery dew.

Mananan was the god of the sea, of winds and storms, and most skilled in magic lore. He was friendly to Cuculain, and was invoked by seafaring men. He was called the Far Shee of the promontories.

BOVE DERG (circa 1500 B.C.)   MANANAN (circa 1500 B.C.)
    son of   son of
Eocaidh Garf,   Alloid,
    son of   son of
Duach Temen   Elathan,
    son of   son of
Bras,   Dela,
    son of   son of
Dela,   Ned,
    son of   son of
Ned,   Indaei,
    son of
Indaei,
    son of ALLDAEI.

The Tuátha De Danan maybe counted literally by the hundred, each with a distinct history, and all descended from Alldaei.

From Alldaei the pedigree runs back thus:—

Alldaei
  son of
Tath,
  son of
Tabarn,
  son of
Enna,
  son of
Baath,
  son of
Ebat,
  son of
Betah,
  son of
Iarbanel,
  son of
NEMEDH (circa 1700 B.C.)

Nemedh, as I have said, forms one of the great epochs in the mythological record. As will be seen, he and the earlier Partholan have a common source:—

```
NEMEDH
  son of
Sera,
  son of
Pamp,
  son of
Tath,                          PARTHOLAN (2000 B.C.)
  son of                            son of
            Sera,
              son of
            Sru,
              son of
            Esru,
              son of
            Pramant.
```

The connection between Keasair, the earliest of the Irish gods, and the rest of the cycle, I have not discovered, but am confident of its existence.

How this divine cycle can be expunged from the history of Ireland I am at a loss to see. The account which a nation renders of itself must, and always does, stand at the head of every history.

How different is this from the history and genealogy of the Greek gods which runs thus:—

    The Olympian gods,
      Titans,
    Physical entities, Nox, Chaos, &c.

The Greek gods, undoubtedly, had a long ancestry extending into the depths of the past, but the sudden advent of civilisation broke up the bardic system before the historians could become philosophical, or philosophers interested in antiquities.

But the Irish history corrects our view with regard to other matters connected with the gods of the Aryan nations of Europe also.

All the nations of Europe lived at one time under the bardic and druidic system, and under that system imagined their gods and elaborated their various theogonies, yet, in no country in Europe has a bardic literature been preserved except in Ireland, for no thinking man can believe Homer to have been a product of that rude type of civilisation of which he sings. This being the case, modern philosophy, accounting for the origin of the classical deities by guesses and *a priori* reasonings, has almost universally adopted that explanation which I have, elsewhere, called Wordsworthian, and which derives them directly from the imagination personifying the aspects of nature.

"In that fair clime, the lonely herdsman, stretched
On the soft grass through half a summer's day,
With music lulled his indolent repose,
And in some fit of weariness if he,
When his own breath was silent, chanced to hear
A distant strain far sweeter than the sounds
Which his poor skill could make, his fancy fetched,
Even from the blazing chariot of the sun,
A beardless youth who touched a golden lute
And filled the illumined groves with ravishment—
***
        "Sunbeams upon distant hills,
Gliding apace with shadows in their train,
Might, with small help from fancy, be transformed
Into fleet oreads, sporting visibly."

This is pretty, but untrue. In all the ancient Irish literature we find the connection of the gods, both those who survived into the historic times, and those whom they had dethroned, with the raths and cairns perpetually and almost universally insisted upon. The scene of the destruction of the Firbolgs will be found to be a place of tombs, the metropolis of the Fomorians a place of tombs, and a place of tombs the sacred home of the Tuátha along

57

the shores of the Boyne. Doubtless, they are represented also as dwelling in the hills, lakes, and rivers, but still the connection between the great raths and cairns and the gods is never really forgotten. When the floruit of a god has expired, he is assigned a tomb in one of the great tumuli. No one can peruse this ancient literature without seeing clearly the genesis of the Irish gods, *videlicet* heroes, passing, through the imagination and through the region of poetic representation, into the world of the supernatural. When a king died, his people raised his ferta, set up his stone, and engraved upon it, at least in later times, his name in ogham. They celebrated his death with funeral lamentations and funeral games, and listened to the bards chanting his prowess, his liberality, and his beauty. In the case of great warriors, these games and lamentations became periodical. It is distinctly recorded in many places, for instance in connection with Taylti, who gave her name to Taylteen and Garman, who gave her name to Loch Garman, now Wexford, and with Lu Lamfáda, whose annual worship gave its name to the Kalends of August. Gradually, as his actual achievements became more remote, and the imagination of the bards, proportionately, more unrestrained, he would pass into the world of the supernatural. Even in the case of a hero so surrounded with historic light as Cuculain we find a halo, as of godhood, often settling around him. His gray warsteed had already passed into the realm of mythical representation, as a second avatar of the Liath Macha, the grey war-horse of the war-goddess Macha. This could be believed, even in the days when the imagination was controlled by the annalists and tribal heralds.

The gods of the Irish were their deified ancestors. They were not the offspring of the poetic imagination, personifying the various aspects of nature. Traces, indeed, we find of their influence over the operations of nature, but they are, upon the whole, slight and unimportant. From nature they extract her secrets by their necromantic and magical labours, but nature is as yet too great to be governed and impelled by them. The Irish Apollo had not yet entered into the sun.

Like every country upon which imperial Rome did not leave the impress of her genius, Ireland, in these ethnic times, attained only a partial unity. The chief king indeed presided at Tara, and enjoyed the reputation and emoluments flowing to him on that account, but, upon the whole, no Irish king exercised more than a local sovereignty; they were all reguli, petty kings, and their direct authority was small. This being the case, it would appear to me that in the more ancient times the death of a king would not be an event which would disturb a very extensive district, and that, though his tomb might be considerable, it would not be gigantic.

Now on the banks of the Boyne, opposite Rosnaree, there stands a tumulus, said to be the greatest in Europe. It covers acres of ground, being of proportionate height. The earth is confined by a compact stone wall about twelve feet high. The central chamber, made of huge irregular pebbles, is about twenty feet from ground to roof, communicating with the outer air by a flagged passage. Immense pebbles, drawn from the County of Antrim, stand around it, each of which, even to move at all, would require the labour of many men, assisted with mechanical appliances. It is, of course, impossible to make an accurate estimate of the expenditure of labour necessary for the construction of such a work, but it would seem to me to require thousands of men working for years. Can we imagine that a petty king of those times could, after his death, when probably his successor had enough to do to sustain his new authority, command such labour merely to provide for himself a tomb. If this tomb were raised to the hero whose name it bears immediately after his death, and in his mundane character, he must have been such a king as never existed in Ireland, even in the late Christian times. Even Brian of the Tributes himself, could not have commanded such a sepulture, or anything like it, living though he did, probably, two thousand years later than that Eocaidh Mac Elathan, whenever he did live. There is a *nodus* here needing a god to solve it.

Returning now to what would most likely take place after the interment of a hero, we may well imagine that the size of his tomb would be in proportion to the love which he inspired, where no accidental causes would interfere with the gratification of that feeling. Of one of his heroes, Ossian, sings—

"We made his cairn great and high
Like a king's."

After that there would be periodical meetings in his honour, the celebration of games, solemn recitations by bards, singing his aristeia[29]. Gradually the new wine would burst the old bottles. The ever-active, eager-loving imagination would behold the champion grown to heroic proportions, the favourite of the gods, the performer of superhuman feats. The tomb, which was once commensurate with the love and reverence which he inspired, would seem so now no longer. The tribal bards, wandering or attending the great fairs and assemblies, would disperse among strangers and neighbours a knowledge of his renown. In the same cemetery or neighbourhood their might be other tombs of heroes now forgotten, while he, whose fame was in every bardic mouth in all that region, was honoured only with a tomb no greater than theirs. The mere king or champion, grown into a topical hero, would need a greater tomb.

Ere long again, owing to the bardic fraternity, who, though coming from Innishowen or Cape Clear, formed a single community, the topical hero would, in some cases, where his character was such as would excite deeper reverence and greater fame, grow into a national hero, and a still nobler tomb be required, in order that the visible memorial might prove commensurate with the imaginative conception.

Now all this time the periodic celebrations, the games, and lamentations, and songs would be assuming a more solemn

---

[29] Greek in the original

60

character. Awe would more and more mingle with the other feelings inspired by his name. Certain rites and a certain ritual would attend those annual games and lamentations, which would formerly not have been suitable, and eventually, when the hero, slowly drawing nearer through generations, if not centuries, at last reached Tir-na-n-Og, and was received into the family of the gods, a religious feeling of a different nature would mingle with the more secular celebration of his memory, and his rath or cairn would assume in their eyes a new character.

To an ardent imaginative people the complete extinction by death of a much-loved hero would even at first be hardly possible. That the tomb which held his ashes should be looked upon as the house of the hero must have been, even shortly after his interment, a prevailing sentiment, whether expressed or not. Also, the feeling must have been present, that the hero in whose honour they performed the annual games, and periodically chanted the remembrance of whose achievements, saw and heard those things that were done in his honour. But as the celebration became greater and more solemn, this feeling would become more strong, and as the tomb, from a small heap of stones or low mound, grew into an enormous and imposing rath, the belief that this was the hero's house, in which he invisibly dwelt, could not be avoided, even before they ceased to regard him as a disembodied hero; and after the hero had mingled with the divine clans, and was numbered amongst the gods, the idea that the rath was a tomb could not logically be entertained. As a god, was he not one of those who had eaten of the food provided by Mananan, and therefore never died. The rath would then become his house or temple. As matter of fact, the bardic writings teem with this idea. From reason and probability, we would with some certainty conclude that the great tumulus of New Grange was the temple of some Irish god; but that it was so, we know as a fact. The father and king of the gods is alluded to as dwelling there, going out from thence, and returning again, and there holding his invisible court.

"Behold the *Sid* before your eyes,
 It is manifest to you that it is a king's mansion." [30]

"Bove Derg went to visit the Dagda at the Brugh of Mac-An-Og." [31]

Here also dwelt Angus Og, the son of the Dagda. In this, his spiritual court or temple, he is represented as having entertained Oscar and the Ossianic heroes, and thither he conducted[32] the spirit of Diarmid, that he might have him for ever there.

In the etymology also we see the origin of the Irish gods. A grave in Irish is Sid, the disembodied spirit is Sidhe, and this latter word glosses Tuátha De Danan.

The fact that the grave of a hero developed slowly into the temple of a god, explains certain obscurities in the annals and literature. As a hero was exalted into a god, so in turn a god sank into a hero, or rather into the race of the giants. The elder gods, conquered and destroyed by the younger, could no longer be regarded as really divine, for were they not proved to be mortal? The development of the temple from the tomb was not forgotten, the whole country being filled with such tombs and incipient temples, from the great Brugh on the Boyne to the smallest mound in any of the cemeteries. Thus, when the elder gods lost their spiritual sovereignty, and their destruction at the hands of the younger took the form of great battles, then as the god was forced to become a giant, so his temple was remembered to be a tomb. Doubtless, in his own territory, divine honours were still paid him; but in the national imagination and in the classical literature and received history, he was a giant of the olden time, slain by the gods, and interred in the rath which bore his name. Such was the great Mac Erc, King of Fir-bolgs.

---

[30] O'Curry's Manuscript Materials of Irish History, page 505.
[31] "Dream of Angus," Révue Celtique, Vol. III., page 349.
[32] Publications of Ossianic Society, Vol. III., page 201.

Again, when the mediaeval Christians ceased to regard the Tuátha De Danan as devils, and proceeded to rationalise the divine record as the ethnic bards had rationalised the history of the early gods; the Tuátha De Danan, shorn of immortality, became ancient heroes who had lived their day and died, and the greater raths, no longer the houses of the gods, figure in that literature irrationally rational, as their tombs. Thus we are gravely informed[33] that "the Dagda Mor, after the second battle of Moy Tura, retired to the Brugh on the Boyne, where he died from the venom of the wounds inflicted on him by Kethlenn"—the Fomorian amazon— "and was there interred." Even in this passage the writer seems to have been unable to dispossess his mind quite of the traditional belief that the Brugh was the Dagda's house.

The peculiarity of this mound, in addition to its size, is the spaciousness of the central chamber. This was that germ which, but for the overthrow of the bardic religion, would have developed into a temple in the classic sense of the word. A two-fold motive would have impelled the growing civilisation in this direction. A desire to make the house of the god as spacious within as it was great without, and a desire to transfer his worship, or the more esoteric and solemn part of it, from without to within. Either the absence of architectural knowledge, or the force of conservatism, or the advent of the Christian missionaries, checked any further development on these lines.

Elsewhere the tomb, instead of developing as a tumulus or barrow, produced the effect of greatness by huge circumvallations of earth, and massive walls of stone. Such is the temple of Ned the war-god, called Aula Neid, the court or palace of Ned, near the Foyle in the North. Had the ethnic civilisation of Ireland been suffered to develop according to its own laws, it is probable that, as the roofed central chamber of the cairn would have grown until it filled the space occupied by the mound, so the open-

---

[33] Annals of Four Masters.

walled temple would have developed into a covered building, by the elevation of the walls, and their gradual inclination to the centre.

The bee-hive houses of the monks, the early churches, and the round towers are a development of that architecture which constructed the central chambers of the raths. In this fact lies, too, the explanation of the cyclopean style of building which characterizes our most ancient buildings. The cromlech alone, formed in very ancient times the central chamber of the cairn; it is found in the centre of the raths on Moy Tura, belonging to the stone age and that of the Firbolgs. When the cromlech fell into disuse, the arched chamber above the ashes of the hero was constructed with enormous stones, as a substitute for the majestic appearance presented by the massive slab and supporting pillars of the more ancient cromlech, and the early stone buildings preserved the same characteristic to a certain extent.

The same sentiment which caused the mediaeval Christians to disinter and enshrine the bones of their saints, and subsequently to re-enshrine them with greater art and more precious materials, caused the ethnic worshippers of heroes to erect nobler tombs over the inurned relics of those whom they revered, as the meanness of the tomb was seen to misrepresent and humiliate the sublimity of the conception. But the Christians could never have imagined their saints to have been anything but men—a fact which caused the retention and preservation of the relics. When the Gentiles exalted their hero into a god, the charred bones were forgotten or ascribed to another. The hero then became immortal in his own right; he had feasted with Mananan and eaten his life-giving food, and would not know death.

When the mortal character of the hero was forgotten, his house or temple might be erected anywhere. The great Raths of the Boyne—a place grown sacred from causes which we may not now learn—represented, probably, heroes and heroines, who died and were interred in many different parts of the country.

To recapitulate, the Dagda Mor was a divine title given to a hero named Eocaidh, who lived many centuries before the birth of Christ, and in the depths of the pre-historic ages. He was the mortal scion or ward of an elder god, Elathan, and was interred in some unknown grave—marked, perhaps, by a plain pillar stone, or small insignificant cairn.

The great tumulus of New Grange was the temple of the divine or supernatural period of his spiritual or imagined career after death, and was a development by steps from that small unremembered grave where once his warriors hid the inurned ashes of the hero.

What is true of one branch of the Aryan family is true of all. Sentiments of such universality and depth must have been common to all. If this be so, the Olympian Zeus himself was once some rude chieftain dwelling in Thrace or Macedonia, and his sublime temple of Doric architecture traceable to some insignificant cairn or flagged cist in Greece, or some earlier home of the Hellenic race, and his name not Zeus, but another; and Kronos, that god whom he, as a living wight, adored, and under whose protection and favour he prospered.

9 781770 831957